AROUND TOWN

BARRON'S

Books in the
WATCH OUT! Series:

WATCH OUT! Around Town
WATCH OUT! At Home
WATCH OUT! Near Water
WATCH OUT! On the Road

First Edition for the United States and Canada published in 2006
by Barron's Educational Series, Inc.

Published by Hodder Children's Books in 2006

All inquiries should be addressed to:
Barron's Educational Series, Inc.
250 Wireless Boulevard
Hauppauge, New York 11788
www.barronseduc.com

International Standard Book No. 13: 978-0-7641-3326-8

Date of Manufacture : March 2013
Manufactured by : Shenzhen Wing King Tong Paper Products co. Ltd.,
Shenzhen, Guangdong, China

Library of Congress Catalog Card No. 2005926321

Printed in China
9 8 7 6 5 4

WATCH OUT!
AROUND TOWN

Written by Claire Llewellyn

Illustrated by Mike Gordon

BARRON'S

We spend a lot of time at home

and at school.

So in the afternoon or on weekends, it's great to go outdoors.

Shall we go for a walk?

5

You go to many different places –

the health club...

the library...

the hairdresser.

In places like these there are lots of people, and lots of things to see.

7

Being out is not like being at home.

Everyone is busy
doing things.

Adults are not always
paying attention.

So it's important to stick
close to them.

Mom?

Or what could
happen?

Getting lost can feel very scary.

You don't know any of the faces around you. You don't know what to do.

Whenever you are lost or feel a bit scared, it's important to ask for help. Who are the best people to ask?

A salesperson

A store employee

The information desk

These people will keep you safe until someone comes and finds you.

But what if you were lost in a busy street?
What could you do then?

You could ask someone for help.

A woman with a child

A police officer

14

Or you could get help in a place you know.

The library

The hairdresser

Don't worry, you won't be lost for long.

15

It helps if you can tell people
the things they need to know.

Then they can call someone to come and find you.

Oh thank goodness Tim is with you. We'll come and get him.

There are other ways of taking care of yourself when you're outdoors. Think about when you go to the park.

Lots of accidents happen in playgrounds. How can you keep yourself safe?

Lots of people walk their dogs in the park. The dogs like to run around, sniffing.

Don't touch him. We don't know him.

Sometimes they want to sniff you.

You need to be very careful with dogs. Are they always friendly?

You meet all sorts of people when you're outdoors. Most of them are very friendly.

I'll just go and ask my Grandma.

Hello. Do you want to see my boat on the water?

But who is it that makes sure you are safe?

Mom

Dad

Grandma

Grandad

Babysitter

Make sure they always
know where you are.

Sometimes when you're playing outside, you feel like an explorer. You discover things you've never seen before.

Always try to play in safe places. Keep away from train tracks and roads. Keep away from water.

Play in open spaces
where people can see you,
or hear you if you call.

You can have lots of fun
when you're outdoors.
Remember to take care
of yourself.

And, if things go wrong and you need a helping hand, always ask the right person for help.

Notes for parents and teachers

Watch Out!

There are four titles currently in the *Watch Out!* series: *On the Road, Near Water, At Home,* and *Around Town.* These books will prompt young readers to think about safety concerns both inside and outside the home, while traveling in a car, and even while on a trip or enjoying the outdoors. The lessons illustrated in all four books will help children identify important safety issues and potentially dangerous situations that they may come across in their everyday lives. Gaining the ability to recognize potential dangers—as well as being instructed on how to avoid these hazards—will allow readers to be more aware of the world around them. Whether at home, at a park, by the pool, or on a road trip, this series offers helpful tips and information on a number of common, everyday scenarios children should *watch out* for.

Issues raised in the book

Watch Out! Around Town is intended to be an enjoyable book that discusses the importance of safety in public places outside the home or school. Throughout, children are given the opportunity to think about taking care of themselves and about what might happen if they do not pay attention to safety issues. It allows them time to explore these issues and discuss them with their family, class, and school. It encourages them to think about safety first and the responsibility and practical steps they can take to keep themselves safe.

The book looks at the many places we go—to shops and parks, for example—and asks questions about what might happen in places like these when someone gets lost or separated from their parents or guardians.

It is full of situations that children and adults will have encountered. It allows a child to ask and answer questions on a one-to-one basis with you. How can you avoid getting lost? Who would it be safe to ask for help if you were separated from your parents or guardians? The amusing illustrations help to provide answers with ideas and suggestions.

Keeping safe in public places is important for everyone. Can your children think of an incident in which they lost sight of their parents or guardians in a crowded place? How did this make them feel? Have they ever been tempted to play in places that perhaps were unsafe and where their guardians could not see them? Are they confident about dealing with dogs? Are they aware of stranger danger? This book tackles all these issues. It uses open-ended questions to encourage children to think for themselves about the consequences of their behavior.

Suggestions for follow-up activities

Make a list of all the different places you frequently visit. What other people go to these places? Who could you ask for help if you were lost?

When might you need to phone the police and what number would you dial to do so? Think up a story in which you were lost. How would you feel?

Draw a children's playground, complete with swings and other equipment. Mark any potential dangers with a circle. How could you avoid accidents there?

Remember to be careful when you're out around town.

Young children need to understand the different ways to keep safe when they're out around town—whether in the park, in stores, or out in the street. With humorous artwork and simple text, this book also contains notes for teachers and parents to help them use the book most effectively.

Text by Claire Llewellyn
Illustrated by Mike Gordon

BARRON'S

ISBN-13: 978-0-7641-3326-8

EAN

5 0699>

9 780764 133268

$6.99   Canada $8.75

www.barronseduc.com

A New True Book

THE MAYA

Ruins of the palace at Palenque, Mexico

PHOTO CREDITS
Root Resources:
© Byron Crader—Cover, 2, 10, 40, 42
© Mary Root—20 (2 photos), 28 (right)
© Lia E. Munson—24 (left), 44 (right)
Odyssey Productions:
© Robert Frerck—6, 17, 18 (left), 21, 22, 24 (right), 26, 27, 28 (left), 32 (bottom), 35 (2 photos), 44 (left)
Nawrocki Stock Photo:
© D. Variakojis—8 (2 photos), 13 (2 photos), 14, 16, 18 (right), 31, 32 (top 2 photos), 36, 39 (2 photos), 43 (2 photos), 45
Journalism Services Inc.
© Schulman—37
Len Meents—5

Library of Congress Cataloging in Publication Data

McKissack, Pat, 1944-
    The Maya.

    (A New true book)
    Includes index.
    Summary: Describes the history, language, social classes, customs, culture, religion, and warfare of the ancient Central American civilization of the Mayas.
    1. Mayas—Juvenile literature. [1. Mayas.
2. Indians of Central America] I. Title.
F1435.M44 1985   972.8'01   85-9927
ISBN 0-516-01270-3   AACR2

TABLE OF CONTENTS

INTRODUCTION

The Mayan civilization covered what is now Belize, Guatemala, Honduras, El Salvador, and part of Mexico in Central America. Most of the Mayan land was forest and mountains.

Much of what we know about the Maya comes from Spanish records. Spaniards came to Latin

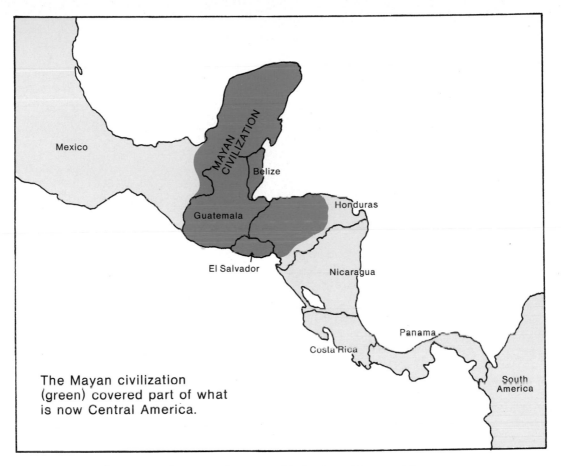

Mexico

MAYAN CIVILIZATION

Belize

Guatemala

Honduras

El Salvador

Nicaragua

Costa Rica

Panama

South America

The Mayan civilization (green) covered part of what is now Central America.

America in 1511. By then the Mayan civilization was already 1,100 years old. The Maya kept records, but most of them have been destroyed or lost.

Ruins of the Mayan city and temple complex at Palenque, Mexico

MAYAN HISTORY

When the Maya-speaking people came to Central America is unknown. The classic period in Mayan history began around A.D. 320. It was a peaceful time when advances were made in knowledge, building, and farming.

The earliest known Mayan city was Uaxactún in northern Guatemala, dating back to A.D. 328.

About A.D. 700 these temples were built in Tikal, Guatemala.

Other important cities were Copán, Tikal, and Palenque. Tikal and Palenque were famous for their pyramids. One pyramid in Tikal reached over 190 feet.

Copán was a city of great learning. Scholars came there to study and work.

Mayan cities in the highlands of Guatemala were religious and political centers. Most common people lived in small villages. They went into the cities only to worship.

It is believed that over-farming helped cause the fall of this early Mayan civilization. War, famine, and changes in climate added to the fall. By 889, the Mayan cities lay in ruins.

That marked the beginning of the Yucatán

Ruins at Chichén Itzá in the Yucatán. El Caracal
is in the foreground. El Castillo is on the left,
and the Temple of the Warriors is on the right.
Chichèn Itzá means "mouth of the wells of the Itzá."

period. The seat of
government then was
Chichén Itzá. The Maya
became more warlike. A
series of non-Maya-speaking
people entered their land.
These outsiders greatly
influenced the Mayan
culture.

Then in 1511 Gonzalo de Guerrero and a few other Spaniards landed on Mayan soil. Several of them were killed. Guerrero was saved by a friendly chief and was treated well. He married a Mayan woman and accepted Mayan customs. It is believed Guerrero led one of the Mayan armies against Hernando Cortés, the Spanish conqueror of Mexico.

THE MAYA PEOPLE

The Maya practiced
many different customs
and beliefs, but spoke a
common language. Over
20 forms of the Mayan
language are still spoken
today in Central America.
Ancient Mayan writing
had over eight hundred
glyphs, or carved symbols.

Mayan society was
divided into several
groups: the ruling class

The Maya wrote with glyphs, or symbols. Glyphs were carved on stones called *stele* (left) and on temple walls.

(nobility), scribes (who knew how to write), priests, craftsmen, and common people.

There was never a king of all the Maya people. Local leaders formed the ruling class.

13

Carving of
Mayan priests

The priests and nobility
lived in the cities in stucco
palaces.

Priests were divided into
four special groups. The
high priest was called
Ahau Kan Mai. He led special
ceremonies and educated

the children of the nobility.

The "working priests" were called Chilan. They conducted the daily worship services. They also served as doctors and helped teach. The Nacon were in charge of sacrifices; the Chacs assisted the Nacon.

Craftsmen served the nobility. They helped build their houses and furniture. They also made the nobles' clothing, including

This carving of a male ruler wearing ceremonial dress was found in Copán, Honduras.

magnificent feathered costumes worn in special ceremonies.

The common people were farmers, hunters, and soldiers. But they all

The Maya plant corn and beans in the same field.

worked in the fields. The
main crop was corn
(maize). Cacao, squash,
beans, and cotton also
were grown. Hunters and
fishermen were expected
to share their catch with
the rulers.

Carved stone heads are
constant reminders of the
Mayan civilization.

MAYAN MEN AND WOMEN

Mayan men wore plain
white cotton clothing. A
nobleman's clothing was
embroidered with bright

colors. The men wore brass and copper cuffs on their wrists and ankles. Noblemen wore gold and silver cuffs. Nose plugs and earplugs were common.

Mayan men burned their hair to form a bald spot on the top of their head. They wore their hair long. Short hair was the sign of a criminal.

Mayan women also wore plain white cotton clothing.

Clay figures of a Mayan lady (above) and a member of the ruling class (left)

They often tattooed the upper half of their bodies. Women parted their hair in the middle and braided it. The noblewomen wore elaborate jewelry.

Governor's palace in the Yucatán

Mayan women served
in government.
Both men and women
filed their teeth and
inserted plates into
their lips for special
occasions.

In this carving of a Mayan priest, you can see the head shape that the Maya considered beautiful.

GROWING UP MAYAN

Four or five days after a Mayan child was born, the mother strapped the baby between two boards. This was done to flatten and lengthen the head—a sign of beauty to the Maya.

Crossed eyes were also considered beautiful. A baby born with naturally crossed eyes was believed to be blessed by the spirits.

To make a baby's eyes cross, the mother fastened a small object to the baby's hair so that it hung just to the tip of the nose.

So that no hair grew on the face, mothers scalded their babies' faces with hot rags.

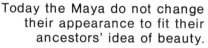
Today the Maya do not change
their appearance to fit their
ancestors' idea of beauty.

Although these practices
seem cruel to us today,
Mayan parents loved their
children very much. In their
culture, they were making
their babies beautiful.

Children were taught by
their parents. Formal
education was available
only to nobles and priests.

MARRIAGE AND CUSTOMS

A Mayan man was married at the age of twenty. His parents picked a bride from their village. They asked a priest to bless the marriage and choose a lucky day for the wedding. The groom's father gave the bride's parents a gift. That sealed the marriage agreement.

The wedding "ceremony" was a big feast. Afterward,

The typical Mayan home has a thatched roof and a door, but no windows.

the new husband moved to his father-in-law's house and worked there for seven years. Then he and his wife could move to their own house.

Each family was allowed to use a small plot of land

Beekeepers harvest honey

to grow fruits and
vegetables. Families helped
one another to plant and
harvest. Each family kept
bees for honey and raised
turkeys and ducks.

Corn (maize) was the
Maya's main food. The women

The Maya still grind corn (above) and live in houses with thatched roofs (right).

soaked the kernels in lime and water overnight. In the morning they ground the corn. Many dishes were made from corn. Stews were made from fish, fowl, and vegetables.

A Mayan house was a one-room stucco hut with a thatched roof, no windows, and one door. Inside was a large room with a sleeping area and a working area. Cooking was done outdoors.

The Maya loved company. A visitor was expected to bring a "greeting gift" to the host. Quarrels resulted when the Maya drank too much honey wine. Family feuds were common.

MAYAN ART, MUSIC, AND DANCE

The Maya loved to dance. During ceremonies and festivals the men gathered in a circle and two dancers performed in the center. Women were not included.

The Maya's favorite musical instrument was a drum made from a hollow log and skins. They also

A young boy playing the marimba in Guatemala

played gongs, flutes, and
whistles.

A favorite Maya game
was *pok-a-tok*. The object
of the game was to drive
a rubber ball through a

Women spin (above left) and weave cloth (above right) for sale in the marketplace. This Mayan mosaic plate (right) is displayed at the Museum of Anthropology in Mexico City.

ring located in the middle of the court. The players could use only their feet, legs, and hips.

The Maya painted murals on every available wall and sculpted statues in wood, stone, and metals. Their basket and cloth weaving was magnificent. They also worked with gold and silver.

RELIGION

The Maya believed the world was created by many spirits. At some time, these spirits spoke the name *earth* and it appeared. Man was created from mud, but was so weak he was destroyed by a flood. Then the spirits sent twins, who conquered evil. The twins were believed to be the

Carvings of a Chac,
a Mayan rain spirit

ancestors of the Maya
people.

The Maya worshiped
hundreds of spirits. Most
of them were nature
spirits. The Maya sacrificed
birds and other small

animals to these spirits.

The major celebration
took place during Mol,
the month when all the spirits
were honored. The Warriors'
Feast and the New Year
were also special times.

Each celebration
was marked by feasting,

The Maya threw offerings into the Well of Sacrifice at Chichén Itzá.

The Temple of the Warriors at Chichén Itzá

dancing, and sacrifices
to the spirits.

The Mayan people were
very careful. When a person
died, a priest had to
purify the house. Bad
spirits were thought to
be the cause of most
sickness and death.

THE MAYAN CALENDAR

The Mayan calendar
was amazingly accurate.
It had 365 days. There were
eighteen months of twenty
days each. The remaining
five days were "unlucky
days." No activities went
on during this time.

There was also a 260-day
calendar used to plan
daily life. Priests studied
the stars and decided

Market day in a small town in Guatemala (left). Masked figures (right) recall the Spanish invasion of Mayan lands.

which days were lucky
and which were unlucky.
No Maya took a trip,
planted a crop, or married
on an "unlucky day."

39

Mayan temple ruins at Palenque, Mexico

The Maya also had a lunar calendar based on the cycles of the moon. This calendar told them when to plant and harvest.

WARFARE

Until the Spaniards came, the Maya were among the mightiest people in the area. The Maya fought one another from time to time, but joined forces when threatened by an outside enemy.

In battle the Maya used bows and arrows, spears, and blowguns. Soldiers also used wooden swords, copper axes, and short

This Chac-Mool, was once used to hold a bowl during sacrifices at the Temple of the Warriors at Chichén Itzá.

lances. War paint was used to frighten the enemy, as was loud shouting and hissing.

Important prisoners were sacrificed to honor the ancestor of a town.

THE MAYA TODAY

Today, the Maya practice Christianity as well as their ancestral religion. They no longer flatten their babies' heads and cross their eyes.

This mother and child and the two boys standing in front of an ancient stone head are descendants of the Maya.

Rural school in the Yucatán (above) and a woman selling vegetables at the market (right)

Most women no longer tattoo their bodies.

But the Maya still speak Mayan languages and follow many of their old customs.

44

Pigs and piglets are sold at market.

The Maya today grow many
of the same crops, enjoy the
same foods, and perform
the same colorful dances that
their ancestors did long ago.

WORDS YOU SHOULD KNOW

ancestor(AN • sess • ter) — a person from whom one is
    descended, usually many generations back

blowgun(BLOH • gun) — a tube through which a dart is blown,
    used as a weapon

civilization(siv • uh • luh • ZAY • shun) — a high stage of culture
    developed over a period of time

courtyard(KORT • yard) — an open space enclosed by a building

famine(FAM • un) — a shortage of food; starvation

glyphs(GLIFFS) — pictures that stand for words or syllables; a kind
    of writing

lance(LANTS) — a weapon consisting of a spear with a sharp,
    pointed end

mural(MYOOR • ul) — a painting done directly on a wall

nobility(no • BIL • uht • ee) — the people of the highest class in a
    country or civilization

priest(PREEST) — a man who performs religious rites

purify(PYOOR • uh • fy) — to rid of bad spirits; to make pure

pyramid(PIR • uh • mid) — a structure of stone or stone and earth
    that has four sides that meet in a point at the top

sacrifice(SAK • ruh • fice) — to kill an animal and offer it to a spirit

scribe(SKRYB) — a person who knows how to write

stucco(STUHK • oh) — a material used for covering walls, made of
    concrete and sand